D0398327

ZERO TOLERANCE

An Employer's Guide
to Preventing
Sexual Harassment
and
Healing the Workplace

BNA Communications Inc.
a subsidiary of The Bureau of National Affairs, Inc.
LEADERS IN DIVERSITY, SEXUAL HARASSMENT PREVENTION
AND BUILDING RESPECTFUL, PRODUCTIVE WORKPLACES

Edited by: Tony Cornish

Graphic Design/Production: Barbara Alter

Proofreading: Theresa McGrail

ISBN 1-55871-354-9

The foundation of a high-performance workforce is a work environment where every individual is treated with respect.

Table of Contents

Investigating Harassment Complaints

Healing the Workplace

Sample Policy on Sexual Harassment

About BNA Communications Inc.

Sexual Harassment Prevention Training Programs

Diversity Training Programs

Training and Consulting Services

About The Bureau of National Affairs, Inc.

Introduction

Sexual harassment continues to torment individuals and organizations. It has damaged lives, ruined careers and left entire organizations publicly tarnished.

And it seems to be as big a problem as ever. Surveys show that the numbers of people who say they have been recipients of harassment continues to grow.

Employers have endured international publicity nightmares — the type of media attention that becomes even more painful as it quickly drives away potential customers, employees, and stockholders.

Even if an employer wins a sexual harassment lawsuit it still loses in legal fees, lower productivity, poor morale, and bad publicity. The only way for employers to win is to prevent harassment from occurring in the first place.

There are many proactive steps employers can take to shield their employees, their reputations, and their bottom lines from the ravages of sexual harassment. It usually begins with enlightened management who seek to change the organization's climate to one of respect for all employees.

This volume is an anthology of articles that have appeared in publications from The Bureau of National Affairs, Inc. and in our publication, the *BNAC Communicator*. Special feature articles from noted experts include Stephen Anderson on *Healing the Workplace in Sexual Harassment Situations*; Trisha Brinkman and Barry Chersky on *Mediating Harassment Issues*; and Karen

Lawson on *Conducting a Workshop to Help Prevent Sexual Harassment.*

It is our hope that this volume will help your organization avoid many of the costly and painful problems that sexual harassment is causing individuals and employers today. As America's leader in sexual harassment prevention training, we also hope you'll consider BNA Communications Inc. your partner in helping to create a more respectful, productive workplace.

Tony Cornish
Editor

From Anita Hill to Mitsubishi

New Approaches Recommended as Sexual Harassment Cases Persist

When people hear the name Mitsubishi these days, chances are cars are not the first things that come to mind. The massive sexual harassment lawsuit against Mitsubishi Motor Manufacturing of America Inc., is a public relations and potentially a financial nightmare any employer would want to avoid.

"An anti-sexual harassment policy on its own is not enough. Employers must educate the workforce about the issue."

Nevertheless, many years after the Clarence Thomas Supreme Court confirmation hearings made workplace sexual harassment front page news, many employers are not effectively dealing with the issue until it's too late.

Sexual harassment is incredibly pervasive, according to attorney Pam White, who represents both employers and employees. She cited statistics that indicate that more than two-thirds of working women have either been harassed or have witnessed sexual harassment at work. The study did not say how many reported being harassed themselves.

White, of the Baltimore-based law firm Ober, Kaler, Grimes & Shriver, warned that employers that have yet to have a sexual harassment problem are the most at risk for a big lawsuit. It is likely they have never updated their policies or their training and are operating under a false sense of security, she said.

Complaints are Still Increasing

In a study by Thomas Staffing Services released in 1996, nearly half (46 percent) of 1,054 surveyed employers indicated they had experienced an increase in sexual harassment complaints in the previous two years, while only 16 percent had had a decrease, and 33 percent said the number of complaints had remained the same.

"When people hear the name Mitsubishi these days, chances are cars are not the first things that come to mind."

Attorneys contacted by BNA disagreed over what degree of blame should fall on corporate America for the continuing incidents of sexual harassment.

Many employers still do not fathom that by hiring strippers to perform at a company party they leave themselves open to a hostile environment claim, White said. White said there still is a perception in much of corporate America that this sort of behavior is okay.

If a company has a large enough staff, "there will be occasional [sexual harassment] complaints," said Judd Everhart, spokesman for the Stamford, Conn.-based Xerox Corp., which has nearly 46,000 employees in the United States and has had the occasional harassment allegation. Although Xerox employees do come forward if they feel they have been harassed, he said, "We always wonder if everything is being reported."

Attorney Stuart H. Brody, senior counsel to the labor and employment group of the New York City-based law firm Gibney, Anthony & Flaherty, said "incredible strides" have been made by companies in addressing sexual harassment. Nearly all employers have at least some type of policy addressing the issue, Brody said. Further, a large number of potential cases are resolved quietly by employers, he said. However, because the settlements are often private, nobody hears about them, Brody noted.

Judicial sexual harassment decisions were intended to address a serious societal ill, but they have had a far different effect, Brody contended. Sexual harassment claims have become a way for employees "to make a quick [financial] killing," Brody said. And employers afraid of bad publicity and going to trial are willing to settle even meritless cases, he said. "This is nothing less than extortion," Brody said.

Policy is Not Enough

A company putting together a policy against sexual harassment must include four things, Brody said. A policy must "state the company's unequivocal opposition not only to sexual harassment, but any discrimination," Brody said. Further, it must define what sexual harassment is. Also, the policy should include a procedure for employees to follow should they feel they have been harassed. Finally, Brody said, the policy needs to state that any harassment complaints will be addressed in an appropriate manner. "If you don't have those four things, you really don't have a policy," he said.

White said employers need a "working sexual harassment policy." For example, she said, a working policy would encourage employees to come forward with any complaints. Harassment complaints are much more likely to be resolved amicably if the employee feels she or he has the support of the company, White said.

In addition, courts have dismissed many sexual harassment claims of employees who made no attempt to report the incidents to their company.

A corporate policy should identify a neutral party to whom complaints can be taken. Merely having a supervisor available to handle complaints often only inflames a situation, if the supervisor turns out to be the harasser, White said. Employers should also state clearly that the company will not retaliate against complaining employees, because fear of retaliation is a major reason many victims of harassment are afraid to come forward, White explained.

White stressed that an anti-sexual harassment policy on its own is not enough. Employers must educate the workforce about the issue, "both their managers and their employees."

Adapted from information published by The Bureau of National Affairs, Inc., 1231 25th St., N.W., Washington, D.C. 20037.

Ending Sexual Harassment in the Workplace

S exual harassment is one of the biggest problems facing employers today, says Bettye S. Springer, management and employment law attorney with Haynes and Boone, Fort Worth, Texas. Because of recent publicity and large jury awards to victims of sexual harassment, the existence of harassment in the workplace is still very real — despite increased caution among employers. "Employers must learn to control the problem in their own workforce, and take measures to successfully defend groundless or exaggerated claims," she advises.

> *"An employee has nothing to lose in filing suit with attorneys who take sexual harassment cases on a contingent basis."*

Steps for Preventing Liability

Employers' first line of defense against lawsuits is to establish a sound sexual harassment policy. Two important reasons for having a policy are to be able to handle a sexual harassment complaint effectively within the organization and to avoid being sued for sexual harassment, says Springer. An employee has "nothing to lose in filing suit," she states, noting that some attorneys take sexual harassment cases on a contingent basis.

Training should be a central part of the policy.
Employers should ensure that their managers and supervisors are fully aware of federal and state employment
laws. An employer can defend itself in a sexual harassment suit against one of its managers or supervisors by
having a sexual harassment training program which was
attended by the supervisor or manager. The employer
then can show that it took necessary steps to train the
manager or supervisor about sexual harassment, she
says.

Managers and supervisors need to understand that
they themselves can be individually liable for sexual
harassment, Springer adds. Do not leave managers and
supervisors on their own to decide what constitutes
sexual harassment, she advises. Establish strict defini-
tions of harassing activities and stress the importance
of front-line recognition to reduce individual and
employer liability.

An employer may be liable for a manager's or
supervisor's harassment especially if it is aware of such
conduct and does not take any action, states Springer.
However, an employer is not liable for sexual harassment
if the employer is not aware of it, it is not brought to the
employer's attention, or there is no evidence of such
harassment.

Signs of Sexual Harassment

"Many employers complain that even though they
have a comprehensive sexual harassment policy, they
are still unable to find out that sexual harassment is
occurring until the damage is done and it is too late for
remedial actions," according to Springer. Employers can
watch for early warning signs, however, including changes
in an employee's work behavior, absenteeism, anti-social
behavior, discomfort around another employee, and
curiosity about the company's harassment policy.

Employers also should watch out for workplace
climates that encourage sexual harassment, such as
swearing and sexual joking, heavy after-work partying

where an employer may end up being responsible for after work behavior, and improper behavior that is permitted on business trips. In general, managers and supervisors should set the "tone" of acceptable behavior, notes Springer.

> *"Managers and supervisors need to understand that they themselves can be individually liable for sexual harassment."*

A Good Investigation

The best defense against sexual harassment claims is for the employer to prove that it adopted effective measures for eliminating sexual harassment in the workplace, and that when it became aware of harassing activities or aware of allegations of sexual harassment, a prompt and thorough investigation was conducted, says Springer.

In investigations of sexual harassment claims, an employer has a problem of confidentiality. On one hand, alleged harassers should be able to know and confront their accusers. On the other hand, alleged victims may not come forward for fear of retaliation or confrontation. Springer advises an employer to pledge confidentiality, although it cannot be completely guaranteed, and to tell employees who come forward, "We will keep the charge as confidential as we can." Springer also recommends that employers remove language from their policies that calls for confronting alleged harassers, because it will discourage victims from coming forward.

Upon receipt of a sexual harassment complaint, employers should tell the employee that prompt action will be taken, says Springer, advising that the investigation begin by immediately interviewing the alleged victim and harasser. After talking to both parties, determine if other witnesses should be interviewed. Complaints sometimes can be resolved by talking to more people and getting a better idea of what actually happened.

Continue to interview until the facts have been established, Springer suggests. A lack of evidence is a significant problem, because employers can be open to defamation suits if they fire or reprimand an alleged harasser without evidence or corroboration of harassment. Confidentiality also must be stressed throughout the investigation — for example, by telling witnesses not to talk to anyone about the charges — because outside discussions about the claim also may give rise to a defamation suit by the alleged harasser.

Finally, Springer suggests, keep all records from the investigation in a confidential file. Never put information about the complaint in the alleged harasser's personnel file. Carefully document all aspects of the investigation and get written statements that can be used at trial, if necessary.

Effective Remedial Action

After the investigation is complete, decisions must be made, says Springer. If the allegations of harassment are true, disciplinary action will be necessary. No matter what remedial action is taken against an alleged harasser, the employer should meet with the victim and explain the findings and the actions taken to eliminate the harassment.

Springer also says harassment victims should be assured that they will not suffer any retaliation. Avoid transferring the victim, she adds, because this may be seen as retaliation. If a transfer appears necessary, be sure to inform the victim of the reasons. Also, warn the harasser about retaliating against the victim.

Even if the claim was frivolous, it is important to follow up with the victim and tell the victim about the investigation and what actions were taken. An even better idea, says Springer, is to ask alleged victims what they would like done.

As a final measure, employers should follow up to make sure there are no further problems. "Even if an employer discovers sexual harassment on an exit interview, follow up to make sure an employee is not leaving because of sexual harassment for which you will later be sued," Springer concludes.

Adapted from information published by The Bureau of National Affairs, Inc., 1231 25th Street, N.W., Washington, D.C. 20037.

Tips for Preventing Sexual Harassment in the Workplace

The most important step an employer must take to eliminate workplace sexual harassment is to have a policy statement that sets forth its commitment to provide an environment free of sexual harassment, according to a staff attorney for a Houston-based energy company.

"Sexual harassment costs a typical Fortune 500 company $6.7 million a year in absenteeism, low morale, employee turnover and lost productivity."

Sharon A. Butcher, senior counsel for Enron Corp., also offered a number of tips on in-house preventive training, internal safeguards and dispute resolution in sexual harassment cases at the 17th Annual Corporate Counsel Institute. The conference is sponsored by the University of Texas at Austin School of Law and the Corporate Counsel Section of the State Bar of Texas.

Sexual Harassment Policy Essentials

"A policy must define sexual harassment, Butcher says. "Use the definition provided by the EEOC," she suggests.

Both EEOC's Sex Discrimination Guidelines and its Policy Guidance on Sexual Harassment define sexual harassment as unwelcome sexual conduct that is a term or condition of employment. *Quid pro quo* harassment occurs when submission to or rejection of such conduct by an employee is used as the basis for employment decisions affecting that employee. Hostile environment harassment is when such conduct has the purpose or effect of unreasonably interfering with an employee's work performance or creating an intimidating, hostile, or offensive working environment.

"It is essential to communicate an employer's sexual harassment policy to its employees."

The policy should describe the responsibilities of management, employees, and human resources, Butcher says. "And last, but not least, describe your complaint procedure and make sure you provide alternatives so that the complainant has an opportunity to bring these complaints to the attention of someone other than a supervisor," who may be the individual the complaint is about, Butcher advises.

It is essential to communicate an employer's policy to its employees, Butcher says. Enron, which has a "zero-tolerance" policy, requires all new employees to view a sexual harassment training film that includes a policy statement from the company's chairman, she says.

Sexual harassment costs a typical Fortune 500 company $6.7 million a year in absenteeism, low morale, employee turnover and lost productivity, the film relates. When an incident involving sexual harassment charges surfaces at Enron, the company acts promptly and tries to minimize damage and restore productivity and work relationships through counseling, warnings, transfers, demotions, suspensions, and discharges, according to the film.

Tips on Prevention

Butcher's suggestions for avoiding sexual harassment include:

- ❑ Avoid reference to female employee's physical appearance;
- ❑ Avoid comments about sex;
- ❑ Avoid physical contact with an employee — respect an individual's personal space;
- ❑ Use appropriate settings when conducting meetings outside of the workplace; and
- ❑ Be conscious that "no" means "no," no matter how "softly spoken by a woman."

"We look at a complaint as an opportunity for us to make sure the policy is being adhered to," Butcher says. "If it isn't, that means we have to fine-tune whatever is going on" and make sure whatever measures are put in place take care of the issues on the table, she says.

Investigating Claims

Enron has three fact-finding objectives in investigating sexual harassment claims, Butcher says:

- ❑ Identify the legal issues and the potential liability of the employer and its agent;
- ❑ Determine the remedial action that must be taken promptly; and
- ❑ Ensure timely, complete, confidential and appropriate documentation.

"We recommend that your human resources representative and your EEO specialist, if you have one, do this investigation together," Butcher says.

When a sexual harassment charge is made at Enron, the complainant does not bring a written statement to the interview, Butcher says. Instead, the company's investigator takes notes, which are later verified and signed by the complainant, according to Butcher.

Human resources specialists and lawyers who deal with sexual harassment cases Butcher suggests, should do the following;

❑ Make sure the remediation fits the type of complaint;

❑ Document the investigation and retain all information gathered during an investigation;

❑ Ensure that all individuals in an investigation keep information confidential;

❑ Keep records under lock and key in a central location rather than in a complainant's file;

❑ Make sure whatever action is taken against a sexual harasser is equitable and consistent; and

❑ Make sure legal counsel reviews the action before implementation.

Adapted from information published by The Bureau of National Affairs, Inc., 1231 25th Street, N.W., Washington, D.C. 20037.

Myth:

Illegal Conduct Must Be Sexual

Fact:

Sexual harassment does not necessarily involve conduct of a sexual nature. Sexual harassment may include conduct that is not overtly sexual but that is directed at an individual based on his or her gender.

Therefore, conduct such as profanity or other rude behavior may give rise to liability for sexual harassment as long as the conduct is based on gender. One such case included, along with other conduct, the frequent blowing of smoke in a victim's face.

Theresa Donahue Egler, a partner with Pitney, Hardin, Kipp & Szcuh writing in
HR Magazine, 606 Washington St. North, Alexandria, VA 22314

Surveys
and
Statistics

.

Sexual Harassment Claims Rise 50 Percent, According to Survey of 1,000 Companies

Sexual harassment complaints, led by an increase in charges of verbal harassment, have risen nearly 50 percent at more than 1,000 southern California companies in the past two years, according to a survey for Thomas Staffing Services Inc.

"That direct verbal harassment is increasing could be an indication of the 'next wave or next level of attention that still needs to be focused on.'"

In its 11th annual employment trends survey of 1,054 randomly selected firms, Thomas found that more than 90 percent of respondents said that prompt investigation is the most effective method in reducing harassment allegations, followed by publicizing a policy, clarifying the definition of sex harassment, a management statement of policy, and requiring two persons for a complaint, the survey said.

Slightly less than 90 percent cited employer condemnation, a guarantee of no retaliation against employees who lodge complaints, defining consequences, and policy reminders as effective strategies.

More Reports of Verbal Harassment

The telephone survey conducted in November 1995 of firms with more than $1 million in annual sales asked human resource decision-makers whether they believe the frequency of sex harassment complaints was increasing compared with two years ago, Wilson said.

Nearly 60 percent reported a decrease in direct physical harassment incidents but more than 50 percent said that direct verbal harassment had increased. Nearly two-thirds said direct verbal harassments were the most difficult to control.

The survey, conducted by Market Research Associates of Irvine, defined verbal sexual harassment as "direct comments about appearance and off-color or risqué jokes." Physical harassment was defined as "unwanted actions that included kissing, hugging, touching or off-color gestures."

Less than 20 percent of respondents indicated that indirect visual harassment, described as the display of sexually explicit posters, cartoons, or magazines, was increasing. Slightly more than 20 percent said it was decreasing, the survey found.

That direct verbal harassment is increasing could be an indication of the "next wave or next level of attention that still needs to be focused on, and it could be employees are much more comfortable coming forward with the complaint," Wilson told BNA.

Written Warning Most Common Sanction

The most common corrective action was a written warning, with nearly 45 percent of respondents citing that method, the survey said. Discharging the offender was cited by more than 30 percent of those responding.

About one-third of respondents cited other methods or were unsure what corrective actions were taken. "This would indicate that many companies either have not prepared set procedures to handle such situations or may prefer to handle each case on its own merit," Wilson said. The least common method was transferring the victim.

Adapted from information published by The Bureau of National Affairs, Inc., 1231 25th St., N.W., Washington, D.C. 20037.

Sexual Harassment Complaints Rising, Prevention Training Not, Survey Suggests

At a time when more companies are dealing with sexual harassment complaints, fewer seem to be providing training programs to prevent incidents, according to a survey by the law firm of Jackson, Lewis, Schnitzler & Krupman.

"Sexual harassment training once every three years or four years isn't enough. It should be ongoing."

In the survey of more than 850 human resource specialists and in-house counsel attending Jackson, Lewis seminars, 92 percent of respondents indicated they handled a sexual harassment complaint in 1995, up from 62 percent in 1994. At the same time, the number of companies conducting sexual harassment prevention training for employees dropped from 55 percent in 1994 to 34 percent in 1995, according to the survey.

"It would seem like the message 'prevention, prevention, prevention' is still not getting out there loud and clear, but it would appear that in the area of sexual harassment, training has to be one of the most important things a company can do on an annual basis—not only supervisors and managers, but the general population" in the company, said Michael J. Lotito, a partner with Jackson, Lewis' San Francisco office.

Recent court decisions in California involving employer responsibility for sexual harassment training for supervisors are "all the more reason why there should be ongoing, aggressive sexual harassment training, and doing it once every three years or four years isn't enough. It should be ongoing," he said.

Lots of Suing Going On

Three out of five of those surveyed said their employer had been sued by an employee last year. The employers of 36 percent of those responding were sued for race discrimination, 35 percent for age discrimination, and 16 percent for sex discrimination and sex harassment.

The numbers are "fairly consistent" with Equal Employment Opportunity Commission figures showing that race discrimination continues to be the most frequent employment suit, Lotito said.

As more companies face employee suits, use of alternative dispute resolution is increasing. Half of the respondents said they use or are planning to use ADR. The most commonly used ADR processes are grievance procedures and internal peer review.

Clearly, Lotito said, companies "dealing with this employment law revolution are going to have to aggressively consider internal alternative dispute mechanisms of all kinds," although no one method works all the time for all organizations, he added.

Companies also need to consider whether they want to obtain employment practices liability insurance that covers such suits, especially since the premiums are starting to come down, he said.

Adapted from information published by The Bureau of National Affairs, Inc., 1231 25th St., N.W., Washington, D.C. 20037.

Goverment Survey Finds Sexual Harassment Still Increasing

The problem of sexual harassment in the federal workplace persists despite progress since 1980 in building an awareness of sexual harassment, and increased sensitivity to the way people treat each other at work, the U.S. Merit Systems Protection Board concludes in its third study of the issue.

"44 percent of women and 19 percent of men complained of harassment, compared with 42 percent and 14 percent in 1987."

Sexual harassment makes victims of everyone because it costs taxpayers so much in lost time, work disruption, and legal battles, according to the study, *Sexual Harassment in the Federal Workplace: Trends, Progress, Continuing Challenges.*

The report follows studies undertaken in 1980 and 1987, as required by the Civil Service Reform Act of 1978, to determine the nature and extent of sexual harassment in the government and to examine the actions federal agencies have taken to address the problem. The report examines the results of an April 1994 government-wide survey of some 13,200 federal workers in 22 departments and agencies. More than 8,000 responded.

The incidence of unwanted sexual attention has not decreased significantly since the 1987 study, the report found. In 1994, 44 percent of women and 19 percent of men complained of such harassment, compared with 42 percent and 14 percent in 1987.

"Sexual harassment makes victims of everyone because it costs taxpayers so much in lost time, work disruption, and legal battles."

Only 6 percent of the respondents took formal action in such cases. The most frequent reaction to sexual harassment was inaction, respondents said, most often because they did not think it was serious enough or because other actions brought a satisfactory resolution.

More than 87 percent of federal supervisors and 77 percent of non-supervisory employees have received training on preventing sexual harassment. About 78 percent of respondents said they knew the channels to follow if they want to report harassment. The report said all federal agencies have policies prohibiting sexual harassment, and 92 percent of federal employees are aware of those policies.

The report (ISBN 0-16-048370-0) is available from the Superintendent of Documents, Mail Stop: SSOP, U.S. Government Printing Office, Washington, D. C. 20402-9328, (202) 783-3238.

Adapted from information published by The Bureau of National Affairs, Inc., 1231 25th Street, N.W., Washington, D.C. 20037.

Myth:
Unwelcome Is Same as Involuntary

Fact:

It is a misconception to say that unwelcome means involuntary.

A workplace affair may be voluntary in the sense that there is no physical coercion, while it still may be unwelcome. In this sense, the victim feels that he or she must participate as a condition of employment. This is most often seen in romantic liaisons between supervisors and subordinates.

To determine whether conduct was unwelcome, the courts examine the behavior of the victim. If the evidence shows that the victim solicited, invited, or encouraged the conduct, a court likely will conclude that it was not unwelcome. Unfortunately, a victim easily can claim that conduct was unwelcome, especially after the fact and after a negative performance review.

Thus, relationships among supervisors and their subordinates should be discouraged. Clearly, relationships that were once welcome may become unwelcome later, thereby subjecting the employer to liability for sexual harassment.

Theresa Donahue Egler, a partner with Pitney, Hardin, Kipp & Szcuh writing in *HR Magazine*, 606 Washington St. North, Alexandria, VA 22314

Policies
and
Prevention

.

Experts Urge Specific Policies to Prevent Sexual Harassment

Employers that have specific policies barring sexual harassment and outlining procedures for handling problems may limit the incidence of sexual harassment claims, according to speakers at a seminar sponsored by the law firm of Proskauer, Rose, Goetz & Mendelsohn in Washington, D.C.

"A formal policy should be accompanied by education and training for employees at all levels of the workforce."

Proactive Policies Are Vital

The law defines two types of sexual harassment, note Proskauer partners, Bettina Plevan and Christopher Wolf. These include "quid-pro-quo" sexual harassment, in which job benefits or continued employment are conditioned on submission to sexual demands, and "hostile environment" harassment, in which the offending behavior has the effect of unreasonably interfering with an employee's work performance. In either case, they suggest, a written, well-publicized policy can deter harassment, or at least ensure that proper action is taken.

An effective complaint procedure, the speakers suggest, should state that offending employees are

subject to discipline, up to and including termination.
Victims of harassment should be encouraged to step
forward and not be required to complain to the alleged
harasser. Instead, a neutral administrator should be made
available, they stress. Finally, employees who file complaints should be protected from retaliation, and their
confidentiality should be maintained to the greatest
extent possible.

A formal policy should be accompanied by education
and training for employees at all levels of the workforce,
they add, particularly for supervisors. Employers that do
not provide effective training "may be less likely to
prevent sexual harassment and more likely to incur
liability in the event harassment does occur," they note.

Investigating Allegations

The investigation of sexual harassment claims should
be "as thorough as possible," Plevan and Wolf say, even
if the victim does not wish to cooperate fully. Statements
of the accuser and the accused should be corroborated by
interviewing third parties, but protecting the identity of
the accuser. A single individual, trained in conducting
inquiries and perceived as neutral by employees, should
be in charge. The scope of the investigation should be
carefully defined, balancing the need for thoroughness
with the need to protect the identities of those involved.
Each step of the investigation should be documented in
a confidential file.

After concluding the investigation, employers "must
attempt to determine whether the alleged conduct
occurred and whether it constitutes sexual harassment,"
the speakers say. The resulting determination, even if
inconclusive, should be communicated to both the victim and the accused. This outcome and any remedial
action taken should be documented in the investigation
file.

A sexual harassment policy should clearly define
swift remedial action to be taken in the event harassment

is found, Plevan and Wolf stress. Regardless of what remedial action, if any, is taken, employers should follow up with the alleged victim to determine if the harassment persists.

Adapted from information published by The Bureau of National Affairs, Inc., 1231 25th Street, N.W., Washington, D.C. 20037.

How to Develop a Sexual Harassment Policy

Sexual harassment suits brought by employees can create enormous hardships for employers, according to Robert J. Nobile, a partner in the New York law firm of Winston & Strawn.

"Prevention and prompt remedial action will be far less expensive for an employer than defending itself in a sexual harassment suit."

Besides jury awards and defense costs, which can run into the millions of dollars, harassment claims can be costly for employers in less obvious ways, Nobile points out. These include the lost work time needed to prepare for and participate in legal actions, adverse publicity, and low employee morale.

Nobile maintains, however, that employers can minimize their exposure to liability by developing a viable sexual harassment policy and effective complaint and investigation procedures.

Guidelines for Policy Development

A policy regarding sexual harassment in the workplace is a must for all employers, Nobile says. At a minimum, he contends, a well-designed policy should include the following elements:

❑ A broad statement advising employees that harassment and other forms of discrimination cannot be tolerated by the company;

❑ A list of the types of conduct prohibited and the individuals covered by the policy;

❑ A description of the organization's internal complaint procedures;

❑ A clear pledge that no employee will be retaliated against for using the procedures; and

❑ A statement assuring employees that complaints will be held as confidentially as possible.

Employers should inform employees that complaints will be handled discreetly, but they should stop short of guaranteeing complete confidentiality, Nobile warns. He cites a case example in which an employee reported an incident of sexual harassment to an executive but asked that it not be investigated or disclosed to anyone. The executive complied with the request, and no investigation was conducted.

Months later, the employee heard about another incident involving the same man and related her experience to the second victim. Outraged that the employer had taken no action after the earlier incident, the second employee sued for negligence. According to Nobile, the employer had no choice but to agree to a large settlement in the case.

The moral of the story, Nobile says, is that employers should never guarantee confidentiality and should always investigate complaints regardless of the circumstances or facts of the case.

In establishing a mechanism for a prompt, thorough, and objective investigation, Nobile says, employers should observe the following guidelines:

❑ Ideally, investigations should be handled by the human resource department, but regardless of who is selected, employers must ensure that the investigation is not conducted by any individual named in the complaint or by any person within the complainant's chain of command.

❑ Investigations should be conducted under the supervision of an in-house attorney or the employer's outside counsel.

❑ All complaints should be in writing to ensure that the investigator will understand the accuracy and scope of the complaint.

❑ In the process of interviewing complainants and their alleged harassers, the investigator should avoid making accusatory statements and ask that all interviews be held in confidence.

If sufficient evidence of harassment is found, the employer has a variety of remedial actions from which to choose. Nobile explains that remedial action has been defined by the courts as action sufficient to eliminate the offensive conduct and to prevent such conduct from recurring. While complainants should be told that remedial action has been taken, they do not need to be advised about the specifics of what has been done.

Regardless of whether harassment has been found to occur, employers should follow up periodically with the complainant to make sure that no further harassment is taking place, Nobile adds.

Nobile acknowledges that some employers may find the steps he outlines for policy implementation, complaint handling, and investigation to be costly. He argues, however, that prevention on the one hand and prompt remedial action on the other will be far less expensive for an employer than defending itself again in a sexual harassment suit.

Adapted from information published by The Bureau of National Affairs, Inc., 1231 25th St., N.W., Washington, D.C. 20037.

EEOC Guidelines on Employers' Duties to Prevent Sexual Harassment

Guidelines on workplace harassment based on race, color, religion, gender, national origin, age, or disability have been issued by the Equal Employment Opportunity Commission. The EEOC's guidelines are intended to clarify employers' legal obligations and would include age and disability harassment, replace the National Origin Harassment Guidelines, and augment the Sexual Discrimination Guidelines. In addition, EEOC seeks to adopt a "reasonable person" standard to determine whether harassing conduct creates a hostile work environment.

"Prevention is the best tool for eliminating harassment, EEOC stresses."

Defining Harassment

Prohibitions against bias in terms and conditions of employment under Title VII of the 1964 Civil Rights Act and other federal anti-discrimination laws require employers to maintain a working environment free of harassment. The proposed EEOC guidelines define harassment as verbal or physical conduct that "denigrates or shows hostility or aversion toward an individual" because of that individual's "race, color, religion, gender, national origin, age, or disability" or those aspects in the individual's "relatives, friends, or associates."

Additionally, sexual harassment encompasses not only harassment that is sexual in nature, but also includes harassment based on gender bias, according to the EEOC guidelines. If the harassment is sufficiently severe or pervasive as to alter the conditions of employment and create an intimidating, hostile, or abusive work environment, an additional showing of "psychological harm" is not necessary.

"Employers that fail to institute an explicit policy against harassment that is clearly and regularly communicated to employees are liable under the EEOC's guidelines."

According to the guidelines, harassment may include the following conduct relating to race, color, religion, gender, national origin, age, or disability:

❑ Epithets,
❑ Slurs,
❑ Negative stereotyping,
❑ Threats,
❑ Hostile acts, or
❑ Denigrating or hostile written or graphic material posted or circulated in the workplace.

Harassing conduct by an employer, employment agency, joint apprenticeship committee, or labor organization can be challenged even if the complaining employees are not intended targets of the conduct, the guidelines say.

Standard for Liability

The standard for determining if conduct constitutes harassment is whether a "reasonable person in the same or similar circumstances" would find it intimidating, hostile, or abusive. The reasonable person standard includes consideration of the perspective of persons who share the victim's race, color, religion, gender, national origin, age, or disability, the proposed guidelines note.

An employer is liable for its conduct and that of its agents and supervisory employees whenever the employer knows or should know of harassment by its employees or agents and fails to take immediate and appropriate corrective action. Whether or not someone is an "agent" of the employer is determined by the circumstances and job functions of the harassing individual. Also liable, the guidelines note, will be employers that fail to institute an explicit policy against harassment that is clearly and regularly communicated to employees, and employers that fail to establish an accessible procedure allowing employees to make harassment complaints known to appropriate officials.

Eliminating Harassment

"Prevention" is the best tool for eliminating harassment, EEOC stresses, recommending that employers take the following steps to prevent harassment:

❏ Have an explicit policy against harassment;

❏ Clearly and regularly communicate the policy, including sanctions for harassment, to employees;

❏ Develop methods to sensitize all supervisory and nonsupervisory employees on issues of harassment;

❏ Inform employees of their rights to raise issues of harassment and the procedures for doing so; and

❏ Provide an effective complaint procedure whereby employees can make their complaints known to appropriate officials who can act on them.

In its existing guidance on sexual harassment, meanwhile, EEOC recommends that employers take the following steps when harassment is alleged:

❑ Investigate promptly and thoroughly;

❑ Take immediate, appropriate corrective action;

❑ Make harassment victims "whole" by restoring lost employment benefits or opportunities;

❑ Prevent misconduct from recurring;

❑ Take disciplinary action against harassers as warranted by the severity of their conduct;

❑ Make follow-up inquiries to ensure that harassment has not recurred; and

❑ Take action to ensure that harassment victims have not suffered retaliation.

For more information, contact: Office of the Executive Secretariat, EEOC, 1801 L St. N.W., Washington, D.C. 20507.

Adapted from information published by The Bureau of National Affairs, Inc., 1231 25th Street, N.W., Washington, D.C. 20037.

Same-Sex Cases Present Myriad of Questions for Courts and Employers

Workplace issues do not get much more highly charged than sexual harassment. And when the harasser and victim are of the same gender, the voltage goes up considerably, as the employment and legal communities grapple with a conundrum that currently has no clearly defined answer.

"Employers are best covered with one broad anti-harassment policy."

The most pertinent question facing the legal community with regard to same-sex sexual harassment is whether, like harassment across genders, it should be covered under Title VII of the Civil Rights Act of 1964. Some say it should not be, because Congress intended the law to protect employees only from sexual harassment by the dominant sex in a workplace.

The courts have so far been split on the issue. In the circuits, only one federal appeals court has explicitly ruled that same-sex harassment is not covered under Title VII, while two have ruled that it is — most recently the Fourth Circuit in a case against Pizza Hut of America Inc. The Equal Employment Opportunity Commission contends that Title VII covers sexual harassment regardless of the gender of the harasser and victim.

Meanwhile, the Supreme Court hasn't been any help in clarifying whether same-sex claims are viable under Title VII. On Oct. 7, 1996 the High Court let stand three appeals court rejections of male-on-male sexual harassment claims.

Broad Policy Recommended

Regardless of whether or not the courts ever get their precedent-setting decision, same-sex cases continue to crop up in the workplace.

Pam White, an employment attorney with the Baltimore-based law firm Ober, Kaler, Grimes & Shriver, said the increase in the same-sex harassment claims is another signal that employees are increasingly aware of their rights. Title VII's expansion to cover sexual harassment "has served to expand employees' expectations of fairness and what is proper conduct in the workplace," she said.

Same-sex harassment is a "trickier" issue for employers to deal with because of the sensitivity people feel about same-sex relations, according to Scottsdale, Arizona-based clinical psychologist C. Brady Wilson.

According to Wilson, many employers' anti-harassment policies narrowly address harassment as something that happens between people of different genders. He suggested a broader policy that covers harassment in all its potential forms.

Employers are best covered with one broad anti-harassment policy, rather than a separate policy covering same-sex harassment, she said. White noted that if employers have separate standards for same-sex and different-gender harassment, they essentially are practicing gender discrimination themselves.

Adapted from information published by The Bureau of National Affairs, Inc., 1231 25th St., N.W., Washington, D.C.

Myth:

Sexual Harassment Requires Bad Intent

Fact:

It is a misconception held by many individuals that conduct must be intended to harass in order for a court to determine that the conduct constitutes sexual harassment. Behavior that may be viewed as perfectly harmless by most men, may, nevertheless, be viewed as offensive by the majority of women.

In recognizing gender differences in perception, some courts have developed a new standard for analyzing sexual harassment claims. Replacing the traditional "reasonable person" standard, some courts apply the perspective of the "reasonable woman" to sexual harassment claims made by female employees.

Theresa Donahue Egler, a partner with Pitney, Hardin, Kipp & Szcuh writing in *HR Magazine*, 606 Washington St. North, Alexandria, Va. 22314

Training

Training Is Key to Prevent Sexual Harassment

The first step to eliminating harassment is employee training programs, say Linda Houden and Larry Demarest, of Dor and Associates.

Before beginning the training seminar, several questions should be asked, including:

❑ Has an incident occurred?

❑ What is the relationship between the alleged harasser and the alleged victim?

❑ Is the workforce polarized?

If the answer to any of these questions is yes, preliminary work may need to be done to vent employees' feelings before embarking on education.

Another crucial element to successful training is a sexual harassment policy that has been communicated to employees by top management. The training session, should delineate the policy and clarify the employer's commitment to carrying out the policy to ensure a workplace free of sexual harassment.

Training sessions should be at least two hours long to allow for small group discussion and role playing, the authors advise. Three or four hour sessions are even better, they say, adding that ideally, training would consist of an initial two to four hour session, followed by additional training programs throughout the year to reinforce the learning and improve communication skills.

Work Still Can Be Fun

Training should emphasize that eliminating sexual harassment does not mean taking the fun out of work. Learning to build respectful relationships in the workplace does not have to diminish employees' creativity or spontaneity, the authors maintain. Teasing fosters intimacy between individuals in the workplace if both parties are participating at an equal level and willingly. However, it must be made clear that it is not acceptable for one employee to have fun at another's expense.

Employees are more receptive to sexual harassment training if it is introduced as an opportunity to receive guidelines for acceptable behavior, to sharpen awareness of their own and their co-workers' comfort levels, and to build a healthy workplace that allows all employees to do their best work.

Introduction and Legal Aspects

Following the introduction, the training concentrates on legal aspects, including recent statistics of sexual harassment claims and lawsuits filed and their negative impact, such as:

❑ Negative public image;

❑ Negative effect on morale;

❑ Lost revenues from lowered productivity, absenteeism, workers' compensation claims, legal fees, and judgments; and

❑ Psychological effects on victims, harassers, and others in the workforce.

State and federal laws and regulations are covered next. The difference between quid pro quo harassment — a request for a sexual favor in exchange for an employment benefit — and hostile environment harassment is explained. The training also delineates employers' liability for harassment by supervisors, co-workers, and third parties, such as vendors or clients, and for conduct affecting non-participants who may be disadvantaged by an intimate relationship between a supervisor and another employee.

Actual sexual harassment cases from the particular geographic area may be used to illustrate legal principles and bring home the negative impact of harassment, say Houden and Demarest. Local professional and amateur theater troupes may be used to demonstrate unlawful behaviors. Small group discussions are another effective tool for identifying and defining sexual harassment. Ideas developed by participants themselves have more impact on learning, the article says.

Comfort Levels and Communication

After discussion of the legal issues, the training shifts to interpersonal relationships. In small groups, participants share their answers about whether they are comfortable with the use of off-color jokes, expletives, or provocative pictures. In the large group, participants look for trends in comfort levels tied to gender, age, race, and other factors. The goal of the comfort level exercise is to develop awareness of different comfort levels and respect for the differences, which helps to ensure a healthy work environment, the authors say.

The final component of sexual harassment education is effective communication skills training, emphasizing assertive communication. Films or videos illustrating different communication styles and role-playing exercises can be helpful.

The training concludes with reinforcement of the use of assertive communication to set limits and with reiteration of the employer's procedures for filing complaints and resolving problems.

In addition to providing effective education and training programs for supervisors and workers, employee assistance programs also can help prevent workplace sexual harassment in the following ways:

❑ Encourage employers to have clear, well-defined policies and procedures;

❑ Balance the rights of individuals involved in the complaint and those of the employer;

❑ Counsel the harassed; and

❑ Counsel the harasser.

("Stopping Harassment Before It Erupts," Employee Assistance, Vol. 6, No. 2, Stevens Publishing Corp., 225 N. New Road, Waco, TX 76702-2573.)

Adapted from information published by The Bureau of National Affairs, Inc., 1231 25th Street, N.W., Washington, D.C. 20037.

Planning Harassment Prevention Training

Training is the best tool for preventing workplace sexual harassment, insists management attorney Stuart Linnick, a partner in Mitchell, Silberberg & Knupp of Los Angeles — a city, he says, where high stakes litigation is the "official sport."

If there has been proper workplace training, an employer that is sued for sexual harassment can say, "What else could we have done?" Viewed in this way, Linnick maintains, sexual harassment training is an investment, not an expense. "Never do nothing," he advises employers faced with a sexual harassment complaint. "Report it, act on it, and don't waste any time," he insists. "Winning" a sexual harassment case means never having the lawsuit filed, not "winning" after waging an extensive and expensive legal battle, Linnick points out.

The world has changed since the Clarence Thomas/Anita Hill congressional hearings, but misunderstandings surrounding sexual harassment still persist and there is a gender gap in the level of awareness of the problem, says Dr. Louise Fitzgerald, professor of psychology at the University of Illinois. Sexual harassment is widespread, she notes. Recent surveys indicate that 40 to 60 percent of working women will encounter harassment. Even conservative estimates indicate that one in four women has been sexually harassed, Fitzgerald says.

"There is no typical harasser," she explains. The workplace culture is the strongest predictor of sexual harassment and the most powerful strategy in combating harassment is achieving a gender balance in the workforce through strong affirmative action programs, she insists. Sexual harassment training seeks to change attitudes and effect a "permanent" fix, Fitzgerald says.

> ## *"If there has been proper workplace training, an employer that is sued for sexual harassment can say, 'What else could we have done?'"*

Effective training requires "fundamentally changing the face of the workplace," agrees Sandra Shullman, president of Organizational Horizons of Worthington, Ohio. Research confirms that sexual harassment is the result of gender and power struggles in the organization, not erroneous mating behaviors, she says.

What to Include

When planning sexual harassment prevention training, Shullman advises that the following issues be weighed before implementing a program:

- ❑ Nature of work issues — including traditional versus nontraditional jobs for women, supervisory roles, and their relationship to discipline;
- ❑ Gender distribution in the work group — including horizontal and vertical distribution, history of gender distribution in the work group and in the entire organization, and the relationship to other demographic characteristics such as race, age, and sexual orientation;
- ❑ Organization/institutional norms — including incidence rates, frequencies, and types of previous complaints, recruitment strategy, and executive involvement in training;

❏ Presence of sexual harassment policies and procedures — including scope, relationship to other policies, and enforcement history;

❏ Person — environment pressures — including pending litigation, community visibility, and perceived risk of training versus no training.

Sexism, the root cause of sexual harassment, is "pervasive, pernicious, and unconscious," claims Barry Shapiro, a management consultant in Oakland, who terms himself a sexist, racist, and ethnically-prejudiced person in recovery. Those who conduct sexual harassment training in the workplace must first confront their own sexism. In developing a training program, Shapiro aims to make the white males who dominate the workforce aware of what they are doing and to see it as so terrible that "they never want to do it again."

"Winning a sexual harassment case means never having the lawsuit filed, not winning after waging an extensive and expensive legal battle."

Investigating Harassment Complaints

Employees have a right to be free from sexual harassment in the workplace and supervisors must be trained to understand that right and to recognize and respond to illegal conduct, speakers at a Labor and Employment Law Section session explain. Prompt investigation of complaints and effective remedial action are the keys to avoiding or at least limiting employer liability.

Confidentiality

Every effort must be made to keep information regarding a sexual harassment investigation confidential to the extent possible without compromising the investigation, speakers say, while acknowledging that confidentiality cannot be guaranteed. Although supervisors have a responsibility to act on harassment complaints, employees also have an obligation to let co-workers know that they find certain behavior offensive, says Claudia Withers, an attorney with the Fair Employment Council in Washington, D.C.

Employers should encourage all employees to come forward with sexual harassment complaints and should establish procedures for resolving charges. The procedures should afford the accused harasser an opportunity to respond to any allegations, and provide appropriate redress and protection to the complainant, speakers point out.

Investigators should inform the complainant and witnesses of their rights to be free from retaliation resulting from the complaint investigation and ask them to report any retaliatory actions. Employers should be careful to document their investigations, regardless of outcome, speakers add.

Union Liability

Unions can be as liable for sexual harassment charges under Title VII as employers, labor attorney Maurice O'Brien of Gordon-Miller-O'Brien, Minneapolis, notes. When the union knows about a sexual harassment complaint, he advises that it process the grievance. The union also has a duty of fair representation to a bargaining unit employee accused of harassment. A union representative should be present during the employer's investigation, O'Brien suggests, so that the severity of discipline can be challenged, if warranted, and to make sure the member's rights are protected. If the union attempts to play a mediating role, it should proceed with caution, he warns.

Adapted from information published by The Bureau of National Affairs, Inc., 1231 25th Street, N.W., Washington, D.C. 20037.

An Ounce Of Prevention: How to Conduct a Workshop to Help Prevent Sexual Harassment

by Karen E. Lawson

The adage, "An ounce of prevention is worth a pound of cure" is good advice for individuals and organizations alike, particularly as it relates to sexual harassment in the workplace. Each year, companies spend millions of dollars defending themselves in sexual harassment cases. Others, lucky enough to have escaped such claims (so far) are taking preventive measures by offering sexual harassment workshops for managers and supervisors. Yet more insidious and pervasive than blatant harassment are the underlying sexist attitudes that often lead to offensive and discriminatory behavior.

Organizations can save themselves money and headaches by taking a proactive approach to preventing sexual harassment. They can attack the root of the problem — sexist attitudes based on cultural conditioning and a lack of gender awareness and sensitivity. An effective means of dealing with this problem is through a workshop which addresses people's assumptions about men and women that often result in destructive practices.

The following is an approach facilitators can use to help workshop participants recognize sexist attitudes and behavior and take steps to eliminate gender-related problems in the work setting. For maximum effectiveness, the group should have an even number of men and women.

"More insidious and pervasive than blatant harassment are the underlying sexist attitudes that often lead to offensive and discriminatory behavior."

The workshop is designed to be highly interactive using case studies, role plays, and small group discussion. After an appropriate icebreaker which give participants an opportunity to become comfortable with each other, the facilitator should begin by explaining that the purpose of this "Gender Sensitivity" workshop is to heighten awareness and practice skills for dealing with gender differences. With this in mind, he/she then introduces the following goals:

❑ To explore the aspects of sexual diversity in the workplace and the impact on individual and organizational goals.

❑ To explore socialization factors that predispose occupational choices, aspirations, and successes.

❑ To identify ways in which both individuals and organizations can deal positively with sexual diversity.

❑ To identify our own and others' assumptions of people based on sexual differences.

❑ To identify ways in which an individual can integrate prominent traits of the other sex into his or her personality.

The first step in dealing with sexual diversity is to develop a general awareness of the problem by defining terms such as "chauvinism" and "sexism" and exploring the roots of this contaminated thinking. One method is to divide the group into small groups of six and discuss representative statements of distorted thinking and their implications. Statements such as the following can serve as the basis for interesting discussion:

❑ "She doesn't need to work; she has a husband to support her."

❑ "Men are so much more logical and rational than women."

❑ "Let's try to hire a man for this position. Men are much more stable."

❑ "I'm so glad you're getting married. Now you have someone to take care of you."

In processing this activity, it is important to stress that sexist attitudes lead to sexist behavior.

Another interesting approach is to explore sex-role stereotyping by asking people's reactions to men and women in non-traditional occupations such as men as nurses or hairdressers and women working as service stations attendants or heavy equipment operators at a construction site.

Other examples of contaminated thinking should be discussed including verbal put-downs such as "girl," "honey," "broad" and sexist language (stewardess, mail-man, etc.). Nonverbal put-downs are perhaps even more damaging since they are often less obvious. Sitting on the edge of another's desk, putting one's arm around another's shoulder, patting a member of the opposite sex on the head are just a few examples that participants might suggest as inappropriate behavior.

After discussing examples of sexist behavior, the facilitator should turn the group's attention to exploring ways in which we have been conditioned through the years to make certain assumptions about men and women.

By taking a look at how our parents, schools, and the media have fostered sexist attitudes, participants can begin to recognize their own limiting attitudes. They are encouraged to think about ways in which men and women are portrayed in magazines, television, movies, advertisements, cartoons, fairy tales, and so forth and then discuss the subtle and sometimes subliminal messages conveyed to us.

One technique is to show a clip from early television such as "The Honeymooners," "Father Knows Best," or "Leave It To Beaver". The group can then discuss the messages being communicated about male/female roles and in what ways we see similar messages communicated today.

After exploring the bases of sexist attitudes, the facilitator should ask the group to focus on the impact of these attitudes in the workplace. Facilitators can also discuss how companies inadvertently reinforce sexist attitudes by hiring female receptionists and secretaries and male mailroom clerks.

A key aspect of this program is self-awareness. Participants are encouraged to take a look at how their own attitudes may contribute to perpetuating sexism. A useful tool is the *Bem Sex-Role Inventory (BSRI)* developed by Sandra Lipsitz Bem. The instrument can be used to explore how one sees himself/herself with regard to one's sex-role identity. The *Gender Impressions Inventory* by George Ford and Kathleen Ford is also useful for this purpose.

Perhaps the most important section of the workshop is devoted to identifying strategies and developing skills for overcoming biases. The facilitator may wish to arrange the participants in small groups to discuss specific actions they could take personally to eliminate sexist attitudes and behavior. One group suggested that men and women managers should take turns taking minutes in meetings and that both genders should open the door for each other as appropriate. The coffee dilemma can be solved by rotating responsibility for making the coffee. The men in the group suggested that they could concentrate on listening more and doing a better job of expressing their emotions. Some of the women acknowledged that they would make an effort to change another's behavior without attacking his or her personality or making moral judgments. Both sexes agreed that they should make it a point to emphasize that successful managers combine the best elements of the masculine and feminine personality and approaches.

Depending on the time available, the facilitator may wish to incorporate some aspects of conflict resolutions, assertiveness, decision making, values clarification and interpersonal communication into the workshop. Modules from the skill-building video program *Bridges: Skills for Managing a Diverse Workforce* produced by BNAC provide useful models for management behavior.

After addressing the skills and strategies for dealing with sexism, participants should be given an opportunity to practice new behaviors. "What Would You Do?" role plays can be used to help them apply what they have learned. Create scenarios such as the following and ask participants to act out their responses:

Scenario: You are meeting in your boss's office with three other managers. In total, the group consists of two males and two females in addition to your boss, Dick Johnson. Dick says: "As you know, we are coming up on the anniversary of the origination of our division. During the past twelve months, we have more than doubled in size, and revenue has exceeded all expectations. We couldn't have done it without teamwork. Since everyone has worked so hard, I think it would be a nice idea if we had a party to celebrate a very successful first year. I would like the two girls, Jane and Maria, to take charge of organizing the festivities." What would you do?

At the end of the workshop, individuals should be asked to make a commitment to change by developing a personal action plan and sharing it with each other.

Although the workshop described focuses on gender sensitivity, the same approach can be used in programs dealing with cultural diversity in the workplace. Stereotyping whether based on sex, age, race, or nationality, is limiting not only to the person cast in the rigid role but also to the person who does the "pigeon holing". Such attitudes limit that person's ability to view others as individuals and as result, impact one's interpersonal effectiveness as a manager, colleague or human being.

About the Author

Karen E. Lawson is president of K.E. Lawson Associates, a consulting firm specializing in organization and management development. She may be reached at K.E. Lawson Associates, 1365 Gwynedale Way, Lansdale, Pennsylvania 19446 (215) 368-9465.

Myth:

Liability Is Limited to Supervisory Conduct

Fact:

Certain types of sexual harassment, such as "quid pro quo," where job advancement or benefits are conditioned on the performance of sexual favors, are necessarily linked to supervisory conduct. But in the case of "hostile work environment" sexual harassment, the offensive conduct need not involve a supervisor or manager.

The courts uniformly recognize that a peer or even a subordinate can make work sufficiently miserable for a superior to create a hostile work environment. This occurs more commonly between male subordinates and female supervisors and might include conduct that is known and perhaps condoned by upper management.

The point is that with hostile environment sexual harassment, the employer is not necessarily "off the hook" simply because a complaint asserts sexual harassment by a fellow employee or a subordinate.

Theresa Donahue Egler, a partner with Pitney, Hardin, Kipp & Szcuh writing in *HR Magazine*, 606 Washington St. North, Alexandria, VA 22314

Investigating Harassment Complaints

Careful Investigation of Complaints Called the Key to Avoid Liability

Amid the confusion surrounding the issue of sex harassment in the workplace, one speaker at a recent Georgetown University Law Center conference cleared the fog with this pivotal remark: "Employers make mistakes."

With that statement, D. Jan Duffy, principal of Jan Duffy Associates, San Francisco, and a consultant on harassment cases, set the tone for her two panel cohorts, attorneys who represent plaintiffs and employers.

John M. Bredehoft, a plaintiffs' lawyer with Charlson & Bredehoft of Reston, Va., said that finding employers' mistakes and exploiting them for his clients' benefit is the fuel that drives his practice. "I live to depose EEO managers," He said. "I will be there to ask you about the things that you know you should have done in sexual harassment investigations."

James J. Kelley, a management lawyer with Morgan, Lewis & Bockius in Washington, D.C., said, "When allegations of sexual harassment are raised, people run around and do all sorts of things they would never do if they simply exercised their good business judgment. You take otherwise sensible, smart, profit-making business executives and turn them into a bunch of keystone cops."

The "first line of defense" for employers who want to avoid the most common mistakes, Kelley said, is to develop a clear and consistent policy prohibiting harassment, and them follow that policy by investigating every complaint thoroughly, and, when warranted, taking effective action.

"I live to depose EEO managers. I will be there to ask you about the things that you know you should have done."

John M. Bredehoft, Plaintiffs' Attorney

Duffy called the need for thorough and prompt investigations into complaints of sex harassment "the new frontier in employment litigation," and listed these steps, among others, as critical to a thorough review:

Planning and organization — Articulate the purpose and objectives of the investigation, carefully select the appropriate investigator or team of investigators, and adequately document the steps that will be taken.

Commitment — Give the investigation immediate attention and high priority, and take action in conformance with the findings and conclusions.

Accuracy and precision — Ask detailed questions of the complainant, accused, and co-workers, and produce a final report, written or not, that is based on facts supported by details and documents, rather than on hazy recollections, beliefs, or feelings.

A timely investigation that is well-planned is essential, Duffy said, because "employers forget this altogether; they leap right into it with 'She said you did this to her' kinds of questions."

"I really think the major part of an investigation ought to be in the planning stage where you identify what is our purpose here," she said.

Duffy added: "Sometimes managers will just assume the purpose is to find the truth and then since they can't find the truth—they know they can't—they kind of throw up their hands and decide they can't do anything."

The goal of a well-organized investigation into a sex harassment complaint "is to try to determine whether it is more likely or less likely that the events occurred as described in the complaint and what the impact of that is in the workplace and what discipline is appropriate, if any, as a result," Duffy said.

Adapted from information published by The Bureau of National Affairs, Inc., 1231 25th St., N.W., Washington, D.C. 20037.

How to Investigate Sexual Harassment Complaints

A dvice to employers on how to investigate a sexual harassment complaint to determine what happened and reduce the risk of liability is offered at an American Management Association seminar in Washington, D.C.

"The purpose of the investigation is not to uncover the truth nor the guilt or innocence of the accused, but to end any illegal activity."

Investigate all Complaints

"The purpose of the investigation is not to uncover the truth nor the guilt or innocence of the accused, but to end any illegal activity," asserts attorney Ellen Wagner, a human resources management consultant in Red Bank, N.J. Once an employer hears of possible sexual harassment, it has a duty to investigate. All complaints should be investigated, no matter how silly or frivolous they sound, Wagner says. She offers the following as some steps to be followed in an investigation:

❑ *Interview the employee claiming sexual harassment* — Allow the complainant to explain what happened without interruption. Probe for specific details, including words said, and gestures or touching that occurred. Ensure understanding by restating the employee's description and getting verbal or nonverbal agreement from the employee.

❑ *Walk the premises* — Look for details surrounding the claimed harassment, including the physical location, date, and time of day. Walk the hall, and common areas — places where things typically happen and where offensive posters might be found.

❑ *Avoid a written complaint at the beginning of the process* — A written statement from the complainant documenting the incident at the early stages of the investigation is typically accusatory, emotionally charged, and inflammatory — simply not useful. Statements prepared after the process is fully explained, however, can be beneficial.

❑ *The investigator's job includes making credibility judgments* — In addition to gathering facts, the investigator should assess the credibility of the complainant. Careful observation of body language, facial expressions, voice inflections, and the internal consistency of the story will help in evaluating the employee's credibility.

❑ *Take written notes during every interview* — Document not only what is said but also emotions and body language. The notes should be preserved in their original handwritten form — including incomplete sentences and abbreviations — rather than rewritten or compiled in a conclusory report. The notes and any reports may need to be turned over to the employee's attorney in a legal proceeding. If a report is required, consult legal counsel in order to prepare a privileged document that will be unavailable to opposing counsel in litigation.

Adapted from information published by The Bureau of National Affairs, Inc., 1231 25th Street, N.W., Washington, D.C. 20037.

Conducting Sexual Harassment Investigations

Sexual harassment is one of the most troublesome human resource responsibilities to deal with because it involves employees' basic values and attitudes, says attorney Ellen Wagner at a Society for Human Resource Management conference session in Atlanta. It is such a pervasive issue, however — from 42 to 90 percent of all working women have experienced some form of sexual harassment — that employers should know what to do if a charge is made, Wagner advises.

Definitions

Unwelcome sexual advances, requests for sexual favors, and other verbal or physical conduct of a sexual nature constitute sexual harassment, Wagner explains, when:

❏ Submission to such conduct is made either explicitly or implicitly a term or condition of an individual's employment;

❏ Submission to or rejection of such conduct by an individual is used as the basis for employment decisions affecting that individual; or

❏ Such conduct has the purpose or effect of unreasonably interfering with an individual's work performance or creating an intimidating, hostile or offensive working environment.

There are two types of sexual harassment — "quid pro quo" and "hostile environment," says Wagner, president of Creative Solutions, a New Jersey-based consulting firm. Quid pro quo (this for that) occurs when expressed or implied requests or demands are made in exchange for keeping or advancing in a job. Because the harasser must have the authority to alter an employee's terms and conditions of employment, Wagner points out, even if it had no knowledge an employer usually will be held liable when this type of harassment is proven. Hostile environment cases may include lewd jokes or comments, displaying explicit or sexually suggestive material, or repeated requests for a sexual or dating relationship. Where non-supervisors are involved, an employer will be liable for this type of harassment only when it has actual knowledge and fails to take immediate and appropriate corrective action, she says.

"From 42 to 90 percent of all working women have experienced some form of sexual harassment."

Duty to Investigate

Employers have an obligation to investigate promptly and thoroughly any charge of sexual harassment, Wagner emphasizes. A proper investigation may limit an employer's liability. "Indeed, in hostile environment cases, a good grievance procedure, prompt investigation, and appropriate action may insulate the organization from any liability at all," she notes.

When and how an employer becomes aware of the harassment can be the key to whether it reacts appropriately. There is no such thing as "off the record" for management and human resource professionals when dealing with sexual harassment, Wagner warns. However, only those with a need to know should be made aware of the charge.

Investigation Guidelines

Employers should treat every claim, however frivolous it may appear, as valid until proven otherwise, Wagner suggests. An investigation should be done within days and should include speaking to anyone who may have personal knowledge of the situation, including the accused harasser.

Make no assumptions, Wagner advises, and confine the investigation to relevant facts. It is important to keep the investigation and the facts it uncovers under "strict need to know rules." Confidentiality is important to prevent defamation of either the complainant or the accused, she says, explaining that disparaging the accused's character unnecessarily may result in nullifying the employer's qualified privilege to discuss the situation during the investigation.

An investigator should take notes during each session with the parties, Wagner says, but should not prepare a conclusory formal report. If a suit is filed, such a report can be made part of the evidence and may prove damaging to the employer. "Let the facts speak for themselves," she suggests. The investigator should prepare a detailed factual chronology, set against a chronology of what was occurring in the workplace at the relevant times.

Reaching Conclusions

Based on all the facts uncovered during the investigation as well as on judgments about the individuals' credibility, the employer should determine whether the behavior was unwelcome and whether it would offend a "reasonable person," Wagner says. The test for whether the conduct amounts to sexual harassment is "the totality of the circumstances" — the nature of the advances and the context in which they occurred.

If the actions amounted to sexual harassment, the employer then must decide on appropriate discipline. Factors to consider are the severity of the conduct, the frequency, the pervasiveness, and any prior complaints, Wagner notes. Finally, follow-up interviews should be conducted with both the complainant and the accused to inform them of the results of the investigation and if discipline is involved, the accused's personnel file should be carefully documented.

Adapted from information published by The Bureau of National Affairs, Inc., 1231 25th Street, N.W., Washington, D.C. 20037.

Avoiding Costly Mistakes in Harassment Investigations

B y following these basic rules, employers can sidestep common mistakes made in internal investigations of sexual harassment claims and possibly avoid costly damages, says attorney Dwight Armstrong.

Armstrong, who is with the California firm of Allen, Matkins, Leck, Gamble & Mallory, with offices in Irvine, Los Angeles, West Los Angeles, and San Diego, recommends that employers do the following:

- ❏ *Publish a policy* — Have a clear policy outlining procedures for claiming and investigating sexual harassment.
- ❏ *Identify the investigator* — Select an objective, articulate representative to conduct the investigation.
- ❏ *Investigate promptly* — Quick action often leads to informal claim resolutions.
- ❏ *Investigate thoroughly* — Obtain information directly from participants without attorneys or third parties present.
- ❏ *Interview the alleged harasser* — Discuss each specific element of the complaint with the alleged harasser.

❑ *Interview other witnesses* — Talk to third parties with knowledge of the events.

❑ *Provide interim relief* — Relief may be proper even before the investigation is ended.

❑ *Take appropriate action* — Review investigation findings with human resources and legal counsel and take appropriate disciplinary action, if warranted.

❑ *Communicate the decision* — Investigation results should be communicated in separate, confidential memoranda to each party.

❑ *Document and retain evidence* — Preserve all evidence for possible litigation.

❑ *Follow up* — Ensure that the matter has been resolved and that there has been no recurrence of sexual harassment.

Adapted from information published by The Bureau of National Affairs, Inc., 1231 25th Street, N.W., Washington, D.C. 20037.

Myth:

Employers Are Not Liable for Third-Party Harassment

Fact:

Employers can be liable for harassing conduct in the workplace committed by a third party such as a vendor or a customer. While these people are not employed by, and therefore not under the direction and control of the employer, the employer can be held responsible for harassment of employees by these third parties. If such situations should arise, managers and supervisors should be advised to involve their organization's human resources departments.

Theresa Donahue Egler, a partner with Pitney, Hardin, Kipp & Szcuh writing in *HR Magazine*, 606 Washington St. North, Alexandria, VA 22314

Healing
the
Workplace

The Healing Process in Sexual Harassment Situations

by Stephen F. Anderson

The Sexual Harassment Complaint

Susan complained to Human Resources about John, her Supervisor, a senior manager. She said that she requested a transfer two weeks ago and has not received it. She believes that John has refused to give her a transfer because she will not have a personal relationship with him. Susan also stated that she wanted a transfer away from John but she does not want him to get in trouble.

> *"Susan was afraid of John and felt that the company gave her no support or alternatives for feeling safe except to transfer her."*

The Employer's Investigation

Human Resources determined that Susan and John agreed on the chronology and general description of what occurred.

John disagreed though with Susan's perceptions that he retaliated against her when he did not give her the transfer she requested.

John realized that he had become too emotionally involved with Susan so he decided to make their relationship business-like. Therefore, he treated her as he treated all of his other employees. He was distant and would give her short answers when she asked him questions.

John did not transfer Susan because he thought that her feelings were hurt because he wasn't as friendly as he used to be and that she would get over it.

John is very upset with Susan because she went behind his back to Human Resources instead of talking to him about her problems. He trusted her and she violated his trust. He is happy to give her the transfer.

Findings

Human Resources determined that John did not sexually harass Susan. He did act unprofessionally when he ignored her transfer request. John's communication style is generally abrupt with all of his employees. He did not treat Susan that way until one month ago when she reemphasized to him that she wanted their friendship confined to the workplace. John should not have pursued a personal relationship with one of his employees because that violated the employer's unwritten norm that supervisors do not date their employees.

Employer's Actions

The in-house legal department wrote a letter that stated that Susan wanted a transfer and that she was to keep her reasons for that transfer and her complaint confidential. Susan signed that letter and was transferred two days after she brought her complaint.

Human Resources met with Susan and John two weeks after receiving Susan's complaint.

John was given a letter signed by his manager that contained Human Resource's findings, a warning to not retaliate, and a requirement that he attend sexual harassment sensitivity training. John agreed with the findings and training requirements.

Susan was given a letter signed by Human Resources that contained its findings. Susan accepted the letter and stated that she is doing OK in her new job.

Analysis of the Employer's Actions, Potential Problems and Their Practical Solutions

I was retained to provide John with sexual harassment sensitivity training three months after Human Resources met with Susan and John. To design that training, one of the people I interviewed was Susan.

The Transfer of Susan

I asked Susan how she liked her new job. She said that she hates it. Susan explained that she only signed the transfer letter written by the legal department because she felt that she had no choice. "The company was not going to move John."

She was afraid of John and felt that the company gave her no support or alternatives for feeling safe except to transfer her. She is angry because she had to lie to her co-workers about why she transferred. She resents John continuing to work at his job while she has to work in a job that she doesn't like.

Susan felt that Human Resources took her complaint seriously, acted promptly and was supportive of her, but that they did not follow up to see how she was doing after she was transferred.

Susan wants to return to her old department but not to work with John. She would like John to understand why she was afraid of him and that she can work around him if he will accept a business relationship.

Susan's transfer to separate her from the (alleged) harasser and her feelings about being transferred are very common. Therefore, be very cautious of transferring the (alleged) recipient even if the (alleged) recipient requests a transfer out of her/his workplace. Usually, the (alleged) recipient believes that a transfer is the only way to be "safe" from the (alleged) harasser.

The (alleged) recipient will be referred to hereafter as "recipient" and the (alleged) harasser will hereafter be referred to as "harasser."

These are a few practical solutions for identifying and dealing with the recipient's concerns and for protecting the employer's interests:

1. Talk with recipients about the impact on them of the harassment, if occurring, and the complaint investigation, their concerns/feelings about staying in the workplace or reasons for wanting a transfer. Explain how the employer prevents retaliation and explore methods and resources to address their concerns in order to keep them in the workplace.

2. Temporarily transfer the harasser(s) during the investigation to separate him/her/them from the recipient(s).

3. Put the recipient(s) and harasser(s) on leave with pay until the investigation is completed.

4. Temporarily transfer the recipient(s) during the investigation, with an emphasis on returning them back to the workplace after the investigation is complete.

It is important to monitor how the recipient and the harasser are doing every couple of days during the investigation.

Other Reasons to Avoid a Transfer of the (Alleged) Recipient

1. Months later the recipient's job or department is eliminated during reorganization and then she/he sues the employer for retaliation.

2. The sexual harassment situation's resolution is focused on the recipient and other employees believe that harassers are not held accountable.

3. The harasser continues to harass other employees. This creates legal and financial liabilities for the employer when it allows a pattern harasser to create a hostile work environment for other employees.

I'm not suggesting that an employer never transfer an recipient, only that it should be very objective about its reasons and to try to first determine if there are other solutions available to resolve that situation.

The following are guidelines for completing an investigation to ensure that it is effectively resolved and that the complaint/investigation-related issues are indentified.

Key Points for Meeting with the (Alleged) Recipient(s) After the Investigation Is Concluded

1. Give the recipient a memorandum that includes:
   - ❑ The recipient brought a complaint (date) and list the behavior alleged.
   - ❑ (Company) did a thorough investigation/ fact-finding and determined that all, some or none of the allegations did or did not occur and that the recipient's complaint does or does not have merit.
   - ❑ A basic explanation of the corrective action, i.e., "the (harasser's name) was appropriately disciplined for conducting unwelcome behavior/violating company policy," if applicable.
   - ❑ State that the company's policy does not tolerate retaliation and to please contact Human Resources if any occurs or if the behavior does not stop (if occurring), or if unwelcome behavior occurs.
   - ❑ Emphasize to the recipient to keep the allegation, investigation, and the corrective action confidential.
2. Has the unwelcome behavior stopped, if applicable? Has there been any reprisals? If yes, investigate!
3. How do you feel about going back into the workplace? What can the organization do to

support the recipient working effectively in her/his workplace (if applicable), i.e., identify internal and external support resources available to assist the recipient, such as teambuilding, conflict resolution, etc.

"An effective healing process helps identify and address unresolved issues, provides closure, and creates a plan for preventing future problems."

4. How does the recipient feel about working with the harasser, if applicable? What do you feel that the harasser doesn't understand about how you feel and about what happened? If they work together, what can the harasser do to create a positive work relationship with the recipient, if applicable? What would the recipient be willing to do to create a positive work relationship with the harasser? What can the organization do to support them working effectively together?

5. Do issues exist with past employment decisions that are related to the complaint, i.e., the recipient of harassment received a low performance appraisal because he/she complained about the harassment, or couldn't work effectively because of the hostile work environment? A new performance appraisal should be written that takes into consideration the impact that the hostile work environment had on the recipient's past work performance.

6. How does the recipient feel about how she/he was treated during the investigation? Note: If the recipient doesn't feel she/he was treated "fairly" during the investigation, she/he probably *won't* contact internal resource personnel if retaliation or sexual harassment occurs. By

"fairly," I don't mean that your findings determined that the recipient's complaint had merit
but that she/he *feels* that you took it seriously
and did a fair and thorough investigation.

7. How does the recipient feel about contacting
the company's resource personnel if further
problems occur?

8. Determine if there are other issues that need to
be addressed.

9. One week, one month and six months after this
meeting take responsibility to schedule follow-
up meetings with the recipient to see how his/
her work is going, are there any other issues or
problems related to her/his complaint, has the
behavior stopped (if applicable), or has there
been retaliation, etc?

Important — If you don't take responsibility to
follow up with the recipient he/she usually won't
contact you if unwelcome behavior continues, other
unwelcome behavior occurs and/or if there is retaliation.

**Key Points for Meeting with the (Alleged) Harasser
After the Investigations Is Concluded**

1. Give the harasser a memorandum that includes:

   ❏ The date and type of complaint brought
   against him/her.

   ❏ The (company) did a thorough investigation/
   fact-finding and determined that all, some or
   none of the (behavior) did or did not occur
   and that the allegation(s) does/does not have
   merit.

   ❏ If the harasser is to be disciplined, indicate
   what the discipline will be and what the
   consequences will be (if the alleged harasser
   is not terminated) if she/he retaliates or
   continues doing unwelcome behavior.

   ❏ Explain that the company policy is to not
   tolerate retaliation and that Human Resources

will follow up with the (alleged) recipient.
(Do not identify her/him unless the harasser
is aware of who that person is).

❑ To ensure that there is no retaliation and
that the unwelcome behavior has stopped,
if applicable, emphasize to the (alleged)
harasser to keep the allegation(s), investigation and corrective action(s), if applicable,
confidential.

2. It is very important that the harasser clearly
know what behavior the employer *believes*
occurred, the basis of each determination and
why it violates the company's sexual
harassment policy or other policies.

Important — At the end of an investigation that
determined unwelcome behavior occurred, it is critical
that the employer be very clear, specific and direct
about what it believed occurred and its basis for that
determination, especially if the harasser denied doing
the behavior and there are no witnesses.

3. Ensure that the harasser stopped doing the
harassment (if applicable).

4. Ensure that the harasser understands what the
organization would consider to be harassment
and what is considered to be subtle and blatant
reprisal actions against the recipient, witnesses
and/or others involved in the investigation (if
applicable).

5. How does the harasser feel about working with
the recipient? If applicable, what can the recipient do to create a positive work relationship
with the harasser? What does the harasser feel
that the recipient doesn't understand, recognize, etc.? What is the harasser willing to do to
create a positive work relationship with the
recipient? What can the organization do to
support them working effectively together?

6. Determine if the complaint/investigation is going to or has impacted the harasser's quality of work and/or work/supervisory/personal relationships. If yes, identify work issues and methods or resources to address them and employee assistance resources for addressing his/her personal/family issues.

7. Determine how the harasser feels she/he was treated during the investigation.

Important — If his/her response is not positive (I don't mean that the harasser has to agree with your findings) identify what he/she feels was not okay and determine if and what steps should be taken to address what was not okay.

8. Are there other issues that need to be addressed?

Susan's and John's responses to these questions identified unresolved issues, highlighted ways to address them, and provided their organization with insights about Susan's and John's willingness to "work out" a process for putting closure to their situation.

Guidelines for Facilitating a Meeting Between the (Alleged) Harasser and (Alleged) Recipient

If the recipient and harasser will work together after the investigation, and you have determined that their work relationship needs to be healed, a meeting can facilitate the healing process.

Important — If the recipient wants to meet with the harasser to talk about the issues, emphasize that she/he is not required to do this. Ask the recipient who would he/she like to facilitate that meeting?

Inform the harasser that the recipient wants to meet with him/her and to have that meeting facilitated by (name of facilitator). Ask "How do you feel about that?", "Is that facilitator acceptable to you?" Ask each person to provide the facilitator with an outline of what each person wants to talk about and to accomplish during that meeting.

Before setting up and facilitating the meeting:

1. Talk with legal counsel regarding what will be documented and in what format.

2. Talk with legal, the managers of the harasser and recipient and human resources about what they will want to know about what the recipient and harasser say, how management will monitor their work environment to assure there is no retaliation and that the behavior stops, if occurring. Find out how they will determine if the healing process is successful and how the harasser will be held accountable if he/she does not stop doing unwelcome behavior and/or retaliates against the recipient, witnesses and/or others.

3. Select a facilitator who is credible. An experienced facilitator has a strong knowledge of harassment and legal issues and is a skilled communicator.

4. Before the meeting write a meeting agenda, identify specific issues that need to be resolved, meeting ground rules, and each party's responsibilities during the meeting.

5. The goals of the facilitated meeting are:

   a. Each party listens and tries to understand, though he/she may not agree with what the other party says.

   b. The harasser takes responsibility for doing the unwelcome behavior, if applicable.

   c. Determine if there are any misunderstandings and identify methods to avoid, recognize and resolve them in the future.

   d. Have them agree on how they will create a professional and respectful work relationship.

   e. Identify communication techniques to effectively and respectfully talk about issues in the future.

Note: If the recipient and/or harasser do not want to meet, don't make them. Instead work separately with each person and have them respond to the relevant key points covered in the facilitated meeting.

Key Points to Remember During and When Facilitating the Meeting Between the (Alleged) Recipient and (Alleged) Harasser

1. The harasser must understand the impact of his/her behavior on the recipient and take responsibility for the behavior, if applicable.

2. The harasser should give the recipient an *unqualified* apology, [if the harasser did unwelcome behavior and the recipient wants an apology.] An example may be: "I'm sorry for doing (specific behavior)" not "I'm sorry for doing (specific behavior) but if you would have told me we wouldn't have had this problem."

3. If the recipient did not do similar behavior, i.e., touched him/her, told sexual jokes, etc., to the harasser, the harasser should not be allowed to blame the recipient for causing his/her behavior, i.e., it was your clothing, you laughed when I complimented you, etc.

4. At the beginning of the meeting the recipient and harasser should be told what is and is not going to be confidential. If the recipient and harasser want something confidential, i.e., only they and the facilitator will know. The facilitator should hear what the general topic is before agreeing to it being confidential. But, the facilitator should state that if the discussion moves to a topic/issue that cannot be kept confidential, he/she will tell them immediately.

5. If the harasser or recipient wants to talk privately with the other party, the facilitator should talk privately with both parties to determine what the issue/topic will be and how the other party feels about having a private conver-

sation. Based on their positive responses and if
the topic is appropriate, it may be suitable to
allow a private discussion. The facilitator
should stay close to the room while they talk
and occasionally monitor the conversation by
entering the room and asking "how is the
discussion going?"

6. Make sure that issues not related to the investigation or allegation(s) which have previously
created conflicts or problems between them,
i.e., performance expectations not
communicated or met, tardiness, aggressive
language or temper, etc., have also been
identified and resolved.

7. As a meeting summary, review the issues
discussed, the agreements made, the communication techniques identified and what will
happen in the future. Also ask the recipient and
harasser "how do you feel about what happened
during this meeting?" and "is there anything
else that you want to talk about?"

8. Immediately after the meeting, talk privately
with the recipient and the harasser to ensure
that what they said about how they feel about
the meeting is how they really feel and that
there is nothing else that they want to talk
about.

9. Tell the recipient and harasser your impression
of what occurred during the meeting and what
you will be reporting to those with a "need to
know" (identified at the beginning of the meeting).

10. Meet with appropriate management and report
your impressions of what occurred during the
meeting, relevant issues, and the recipient's and
harasser's agreements. Management should
initiate the action plan for the responsible

parties, i.e., the harasser's direct supervisor, HR, legal department, etc., to document the healing process and to monitor the harasser and recipient.

As a result of their facilitated meeting, John agreed to have Susan transferred back to his department, but she would work for another manager. Susan and John agreed upon a comfortable way to interact when they saw each other. Susan is happy to be working in her former department with her friends. John understands why Susan was afraid of him and is comfortable seeing her around his department. John and Susan feel that for the first time they really had a chance to talk about how they felt, the issues, and that they were really listened to. Because of that they are able to put closure to what happened.

An effective healing process helps identify unresolved issues, resolves issues, provides the parties involved with closure, creates a plan for preventing future problems and emphasizes that the parties take responsibility for what they individually did and for the healing process.

(This *process* is not inclusive nor legal advice.)

About the Author

Stephen Anderson is president of Anderson-davis Inc. of Denver, Colorado. Stephen is retained as an expert witness and consults on how to heal workplaces. He also provides one-on-one coaching/training for accused harassers. He has designed and delivered training programs on diversity, gender, sexual harassment, management, healing workplaces, and conflict resolution since 1972 for more than 120,000 employees in the U.S., Japan, and Canada. Stephen provides train-the-trainer consulting and training on how to implement effective in-house sexual harassment training programs. For more information about his training programs and consulting services, call (303) 699-7074.

Stephen is the author of **How to Effectively Manage Sexual Harassment Investigations** and is the creator of **Intent vs. Impact** (available in Spanish) and **Myths vs. Facts**, (available in Spanish and French), two of the most popular video-based sexual harassment prevention training programs ever produced and **Respect vs. Harassment**, a new video-based program that shows employees how to prevent all types of harassment and helps supervisors resolve harassment situations and heal the workplace. For information call 1-800-233-6067.

Creative Resolutions: Mediating Sexual Harassment Issues

by Barry Chersky and Trisha Brinkman

"I don't want to make a big deal out of it, I just want him to stop asking me out."

"I don't think she means anything by it, but I feel uncomfortable when she touches my shoulder every time she greets me."

"I want to have a productive, professional working relationship, and I'm afraid if I say something, especially if I make a complaint, things will get worse."

"I'm sorry I ever spoke up. Now that the company did their investigation, it feels more awkward than ever."

The awareness of sexual harassment is heightening and employers are being held to increasingly higher standards for maintaining an environment free of sexual harassment and for effectively resolving possible sexual harassment situations. In the face of these trends, organizations are looking for a broader range of methods to avoid potential liability and maintain work environments that are comfortable for all employees.

Employers are experimenting with creative alternatives to the more formal approaches of resolving sexual harassment situations and, in many cases, are finding success. Recognizing each situation must be handled on a case-by-case basis, the nature and severity of the allegations, the working relationship of the involved parties, and the particularities of the circumstances will dictate the appropriate response. In many cases, a more informal approach may lead to the most effective resolution.

"Mediation can help minimize problems encountered in resolving sexual harassment situations."

Alternative dispute resolution (ADR), which includes mediation, is a new and growing field which, in the appropriate situation, can successfully be applied to sexual harassment issues. Mediation, as an alternative to, or in the aftermath of, a formal investigation can help to minimize if not eliminate many of the problems encountered by employers who use more traditional methods of resolution.

The basic goal of mediation is to facilitate a negotiation process between the parties to effectively define a desired outcome, thereby resolving conflict. In the case of sexual harassment which, in nearly every instance, involves an imbalance of power, the goal of mediation typically is aimed at one or more of the following:

- ❑ to provide a controlled and safe opportunity for each party to express his/her perspective of the situation and feel heard;
- ❑ to have the party who has engaged in offensive behavior understand the impact of the conduct and, if desired by the recipient, offer an apology;
- ❑ to define the parameters of a mutually respectful work relationship in order to proceed into the

future rather than focus on the past or, more
simply put;

❑ to negotiate an appropriate remedy to the
situation.

Assessing Mediation as an Option

Before deciding on implementing an alternative
resolution strategy it is critically important that the
employer conduct a thorough assessment to determine
the appropriateness of such an option. In order for
mediation to be successful the process must be voluntary
for all parties involved, one to which they are open and,
most importantly, confidential.

Above all else, the recipient of the alleged harassment
must not feel coerced or pressured to participate in the
mediation. The vast majority of people who experience
sexual harassment remain hesitant to complain about
the behavior for fear of retaliation, among other reasons.
Therefore, a careful appraisal must first be conducted
with the recipient of the harassment to ensure that she,
or sometimes he, can freely participate in the mediation
without fear of reprisal.

Beyond these factors, there are additional consider-
ations to explore before using mediation as a resolution
strategy. Is the situation mediable? That is, can an
honest resolution truly be mediated? If the accused has
a history of harassing behavior or agrees to participate at
the employers request only to avoid further corrective
action or, if after an investigation there has been a clear
finding that the harassment policy has been violated,
mediation would most often not be the appropriate
alternative.

However, in many situations, for example, when the
behavior was perceived differently by the parties, when
intent has been misconstrued, when the conduct was
subtle and an isolated occurrence, or when there has

been genuine miscommunication, mediation can often provide the most effective resolution.

How Mediation Can Work

If the assessment indicates that conditions are appropriate to proceed with mediation, it will be important to ascertain who will facilitate the process, and who will be present. Because each situation is unique, there is no one correct way to make this determination.

In terms of selection of a facilitator, there are potential advantages and disadvantages of using either an internal or external mediator. The most obvious benefit of using someone outside of the organization is the greater possibility that this individual will be perceived as more credible, neutral and unbiased, without an interest in any particular outcome. However, because an external mediator will most likely be unknown to the parties, there initially might be heightened discomfort. Conversely, an internal facilitator might engender a higher level of comfort due to familiarity, while raising concerns about neutrality.

Regardless of whether the facilitator is external or internal it is critical this person has a clear understanding of mediation principles, has a clear understanding of sexual harassment related issues, is credible, and is able to guarantee confidentiality of the process.

In some situations, co-mediators might be the ideal choice. For example, if the conflict exists between a woman and a man, a male-female team of mediators might present the most productive method for resolution.

In particular circumstances, for example, when the complainant has been traumatized but remains open to more informal resolution, shuttle mediation, in which the mediator works with each party separately, might prove to be the preferred option. In such a situation, the mediator might ask the complaining party to put her or his wishes in writing and, with the use of that document, negotiate a resolution with the other party.

Mediation in these circumstances is being used as an alternative method of fulfilling the employer's obligation to take action when knowledge of a potential harassment situation exists. Therefore, it is imperative that a company representative be involved to ensure that the process is both a suitable as well as effective response. In most cases, while it would not be appropriate for such a representative to be present in the initial individual interviews (unless that person will be conducting the mediation), it would be proper to attend any or all of the mediation sessions, particularly the final session/s where agreement between the parties is hopefully reached. The employer is ultimately responsible to hold all employees accountable to the company policy prohibiting harassment and, in this case, to any agreement that is attained as a result of the mediation process.

Rationale for Mediation

While preventive measures, such as adopting and strictly enforcing strong anti-harassment policies and providing training to all managers and employees can be the most effective tools for addressing the issue, organizations still have the challenge of managing sexual harassment situations when they occur. Organizations that have experienced the time-consuming, resource-draining, and often costly experience of conducting an investigation and implementing corrective action, know the formal resolution process often fails to truly resolve the issue. While the employer's legal obligations may have technically been met, the very process itself could produce an even longer list of problems.

The complainant may feel further traumatized by the invasive and often embarrassing nature of the investigation. The alleged harasser may feel victimized. The rumor mill can exacerbate the situation, affecting greater numbers of employees and negatively impacting morale and productivity while increasing hostility and animosity. Despite efforts to limit the scope of the investigation and minimize the number of parties involved, it is the rare organization that can assure the level of confidentiality that prevents knowledge of the situation from being spread throughout the workplace.

If the complaint cannot be substantiated, the matter could even worsen. When there is a finding that a violation has occurred, and the parties must continue to work with each other, life can be miserable not only for the individuals directly involved, but also for others with whom they work. Doing traditional fact-findings or investigations does not guarantee a successful resolution.

While mediation does not guarantee effective resolution in all circumstances nor does it relieve the employer of its duty to investigate complaints, as necessary, and ensure appropriate remedial action, it offers a viable alternative to the more traditional methods of corrective action and resolution.

About the Authors

Trisha Brinkman and Barry Chersky, of Brinkman & Chersky Consulting offer training programs on recognizing and resolving sexual harassment, as well as mediation and investigation services. Both have served as expert witnesses on over 50 sexual harassment court cases. They are the co-authors of ***Changing Boundaries: Recognizing, Preventing and Resolving Sexual Harassment,*** a video-supported training program distributed by BNAC. For information, call BNAC at 1-800-233-6067.

To contact Brinkman and Chersky Consulting call (415) 661-4040. Address: 1300 12th Avenue, San Francisco, CA 94122.

Sample Policy on Sexual Harassment

To: All Employees

Re: Policy on Sexual Harassment

Sexual harassment is illegal and against the policies of this Organization.

Sexual harassment involves (a) making unwelcomed sexual advances or requests for sexual favors or other verbal or physical conduct of a sexual nature a condition of employment, or (b) making submission to or rejection of such conduct the basis for employment decisions, or (c) creating an intimidating, offensive, or hostile working environment by such conduct.

The following are examples of sexual harassment:

❑ *Verbal:* Sexual innuendo, suggestive comments, insults, threats, jokes about gender-specific traits, or sexual propositions;

❑ *Nonverbal:* Making suggestive or insulting noises, leering, whistling, or making obscene gestures; and

❑ *Physical:* Touching, pinching, brushing the body, coercing sexual intercourse, or assault.

Any employee who believes he or she has been the subject of sexual harassment should report the alleged conduct immediately to Mr. X or Ms. Y in the Personnel Department. A confidential investigation of any complaint will be undertaken immediately.

Any employee found by the Organization to have sexually harassed another employee will be subject to appropriate disciplinary sanctions ranging from a warning in his or her file up to and including termination.

Retaliating or discriminating against an employee for complaining about sexual harassment is prohibited.

The Organization recognizes that the issue of whether sexual harassment has occurred requires a factual determination based on all the evidence received. The Company also recognizes that false accusations of sexual harassment can have serious effects on innocent men and women. We trust that all employees will continue to act in a responsible and professional manner to establish a pleasant working environment free of discrimination.

About BNA Communications Inc.
The Leader in Diversity, Sexual Harassment Prevention, and Building Respectful, Productive Workplaces

BNA Communications Inc., a subsidiary of The Bureau of National Affairs, Inc., is America's leader in sexual harassment prevention training with the largest selection of products and services of any organization. BNA Communications is a provider of human resource and employment law training to nine out of ten FORTUNE 500 corporations, government agencies and many other employers large and small. More organizations get their sexual harassment prevention training from BNAC than from any other training provider.

By combining the legal and information resources of BNA with the training expertise of award-winning course designers, video producers and nationally-recognized consultants, we are uniquely qualified to bring you accurate and effective instruction that gets results you can rely on.

Call your BNAC training consultant to discuss how our training programs can help you achieve your business goals. Call 1-800-233-6067 today.

Sexual Harassment Prevention Training Programs
Respect vs. Harassment

Harassing someone because of their sex, race, ethnicity, religion, weight, sexual orientation, etc., and other types of harassment such as an emotionally abusive manager, can result in substantial liability and/or workplace conflict for employers and employees. This new two video-supported training program assists all employees in preventing and resolving harassment and shows managers how to effectively manage harassment complaints and rebuild productive work relationships.

Training Objectives:

❑ Dramatizes a wide variety of blatant to subtle harassment behaviors;

❑ Shows employees methods for preventing and resolving workplace harassment;

❑ Provides managers with skills to prevent, recognize and resolve harassment and retaliation situations;

❑ Demonstrate techniques to investigate harassment situations and to heal the workplaces impacted by the complaint and/or investigation.

Support Material: Trainer's Manual; Participant Manual for Each Module.

Myths vs. Facts

Stephen Anderson, (one of America's foremost experts on sexual harassment prevention), hosts this comprehensive video-supported training program on sexual harassment prevention.

Training Objectives:

❑ Show the line between flirtation and subtle sexual harassment;

❑ Illustrate a wide variety of harassment scenarios including same-sex, female-to-male, and third party;

❑ Present a practical five-step method for identifying subtle sexual harassment;

❑ Detail the responsibilities of managers to intervene in harassment situations;

❏ Show managers how to interview alleged recipients of sexual harassment and confront harassers.

Support Material: 250-page Trainer's Manual; Participant Manuals for Each Module; 342-page Resource Book "How to Effectively Manage Sexual Harassment Situations."

Preventing Sexual Harassment

This two-part video-supported training program establishes the consequences of sexual harassment in the workplace for all employee and clearly outlines the responsibilities of managers to prevent it.

Training Objectives:

❏ Show what harassment is and what distinguishes it from friendly behavior;

❏ Demonstrate the employer's commitment to prevent harassment;

❏ Illustrate internal complaint procedures;

❏ Encourage employees to resolve complaints internally;

❏ Outline managers' responsibilities for maintaining a harassment-free workplace;

❏ Show how to investigate sexual harassment complaints.

Support Material: 140-page Trainer's Manual; Management and Employee Participant Manuals.

Working with People: A Personal Responsibility Guide for Preventing Sexual Harassment

This video-supported training program helps get employees involved in creating a harassment-free workplace and shows that prohibitions against sexual harassment also apply at off-site business functions.

Training Objectives:

❑ Explain little-known aspects of sexual harassment laws;

❑ Show trainees how to take personal responsibility for preventing harassment;

❑ Highlight proper business etiquette and skills for working with people at off-site business functions;

❑ Reinforce that the organization expects professional behavior at off-site business functions.

Support Material: Trainer's Manual; Participant Manuals.

Sexual Harassment Plain and Simple

Featuring 19 different vignettes of harassment situations, this two-part video-supported training program offers a powerful set of real-life situations to provide training on sexual harassment in easy-to-understand, non-legalistic terms.

Training Objectives:

❑ Clearly define what sexual harassment is;

❑ Show employees how they can resolve situations themselves;

❑ Provide clear instructions on how to report harassment incidents;

❑ Encourage internal reporting of harassment situations.

Support Material: Leader's Guide, Participant Booklets.

Changing Boundaries:
Recognizing, Preventing and Resolving Sexual Harassment

Trisha Brinkman and Barry Chersky, (nationally-recognized authorities in sexual harassment prevention), host this in-depth exploration of sexual harassment in the workplace. Excellent for self-study by individuals or groups.

Training Objectives:

❑ Increase understanding of the subtleties of sexual harassment;

❑ Illustrate and define inappropriate behaviors;

❑ Show employees how to maintain a work environment free of harassment;

❑ Define the legal responsibilities of managers and the organization;

❑ Prepare managers to receive complaints and resolve harassment situations.

Support Material: 124-page Trainer's Manual; Management and Employee Participant Manuals.

Intent vs. Impact

One of the most widely-used programs of its kind, *Intent vs. Impact* covers what your managers and employees need to know to protect your organization from sexual harassment liability. Includes separate video-supported training programs for managers and employees.

Training Objectives:

❑ Show the fine line between flirtation and harassment;

❑ Define hostile work environment and *quid pro quo* harassment;

❑ Show managers how to receive complaints, confront harassers, and resolve harassment situations;

❑ Demonstrate how employees can put a stop to unwanted behavior;

❑ Highlight EEOC guidelines, Title IX and Executive Order 11246 requirements.

Support Material: 116-page Trainer's Manual; Management and Employee Participant Manuals.

Crossing the Line

This video-supported training program shows managers and employees how to prevent sexual harassment in hospitality workplaces such as hotels, restaurants, airports, and other service environments.

Training Objectives:

❑ Provide a clear definition of sexual harassment;

❑ Examine the responsibilities and potential liabilities of the organization;

❑ Explore techniques for managing harassment in the workplace.

Support Material: 72-page Trainer's Manual; Participant Manual.

A Costly Proposition:
Sexual Harassment at Work

This video-supported training program features five dramatic vignettes each addressing a different area of sexual harassment. It includes three separate learning designs to facilitate training for managers, employees, and human resource professionals in a powerful instructor-led workshop. The video features many well-known character actors including Wesley Snipes.

Training Objectives:

❑ Provide your employees with a clear definition
of harassment and its legal implications for your
organization;

❑ Explore sexual harassment issues as they relate
to working relationships within your
organization;

❑ Examine immediate and long-term preventive
solutions your employees can use to deal with
the issue.

Support Material: 144-page Trainer's Manual; Participant Manual.

Jack Cade's Nightmare:
A Supervisor's Guide to Laws Affecting the Workplace

This video-supported training program shows managers and supervisors how to avoid legal mistakes in
today's highly-litigious society.

Training Objectives:

❑ Provide an introduction to the most common
legal pitfalls that can trip up even the most
careful supervisors;

❑ Show how to spot potential problems and avoid
mistakes that can cause legal liability for the
organization and managers personally;

❑ Present ten simple rules that can avoid trouble.

Support Material: 54-page Trainer's Manual; Participant's Manuals.

Double Liability:
A Guide to Managing Conflict in the Workplace

Organizations may be held liable for conflicts between and among employees should their supervisors fail to remedy the situation. This video-supported training program gives managers the skills and awareness to prevent legal liability resulting from workplace conflicts such as sex-, race-, and AIDS-based harassment, workplace violence, defamation, e-mail abuse, and alcohol and drug abuse.

Training Objectives:

❑ Illustrate the most common legal pitfalls that can stem from workplace conflicts;

❑ Show managers that, in addition to liability for their own inappropriate actions or statements, they may be held liable for those of their employees;

❑ Provide guidance on how to spot problems and avoid mistakes commonly made by managers concerning workplace conflicts.

Support Material: Trainer's Manual; Participant Manual.

Diversity Training Programs

BNA Communications Inc. is also the leader in diversity training programs with the widest selection of training programs and consulting services of any training provider.

Diversity: The Competitive Advantage

This video-supported training program unites diversity, empowerment, and teamwork to help create the high-performance organization of the 21st Century.

Training Objectives:
- ❑ Define diversity and show how it is related to creating a high-performance organization;
- ❑ Create proactive strategies for eliminating barriers where intergroup differences exist;
- ❑ Show that diversity and empowerment are inseparable initiatives that are necessary to create an efficient and successful organization;
- ❑ Demonstrate the interpersonal skills necessary to work effectively on diverse cross-cultural teams.

Support Material: Trainer's Manual; Participant's Manuals; "The Business of Diversity" books.

Brainwaves: Case Studies in Diversity

A state-of-the-art video-supported training program, *Brainwaves* examines perceptions and thinking patterns to help all employees become responsible for valuing and respecting differences in the workplace.

Training Objectives:
- ❑ Increase awareness of perceptions and thinking patterns and how they influence relationships in a diverse workplace;
- ❑ Build skills and motivation that will help maintain effective work relationships based on a respect for differences and a recognition of common interests;
- ❑ Recognize and respect individual rights in a diverse workplace.

Support Material: 212-page Trainer's Manual; Participant Manuals for Each Module.

A Winning Balance

The standard for quality in diversity training, *A Winning Balance* helps all employees explore their own attitudes about those who are different and shows how diversity can benefit individuals and the organization.

Training Objectives:

❑ Introduce the topic of diversity and show why it is important to the organization;

❑ Help trainees explore their own personal attitudes towards those who are different using a unique instructional tool known as the "tolerance scale";

❑ Show the impact of biases and stereotypes using interviews with real people;

❑ Explore what employees can do to become a "change agent" for diversity.

Support Materials: 52-page Trainer's Manual; Participant Manuals; "Commitment to Diversity" Banner; Photo Cards.

Produced by PROgroup®.

Smarter Together:
Insights Into Male/Female Interactions

This video-supported training program helps trainees gain an understanding of gender differences and learn skills that enhance communication, teamwork, morale, and productivity.

Training Objectives:

❑ Explore the differences between men and women and how they impact relationships at work;

❑ Provide insight into male/female communication styles;

❑ Illustrate ways to resolve conflicts between men and women;

❑ Show employees how to work together more effectively by appreciating gender differences.

Support Material: Trainer's Manual; Participant Manuals.

Produced in cooperation with PROgroup®.

The Cost of Intolerance

Biases and stereotypes can cost business and lead to legal trouble. This video-supported training program helps improve customer service and increase sales by eliminating intolerant attitudes from frontline service and sales people.

Training Objectives:

❑ Show employees the lost business opportunities resulting from intolerance toward customers of differing race, sex, age, religion, ethnic background, ability/disability or sexual orientation.

❑ Build understanding of how attitudes, biases, and assumptions toward customers impact the quality of service;

❑ Help trainees develop a personal awareness of the "service energy" they provide;

❑ Enhance compliance with various government regulations in banking, mortgage lending, insurance, and other industries.

Support Material: 52-page Trainer's Manual; Participant Manuals; "Service Energy" Assessment Tests.

Produced in cooperation with PROgroup®.

BRIDGES:
Skills for Managing a Diverse Workforce

Managing diversity requires more than awareness. This eight-module video-supported training program provides managers and supervisors with solid skills to help your organization make workforce diversity a competitive edge.

Training Objectives:

❑ Develop and reinforce an awareness of diversity;

❑ Illustrate skills for giving and receiving feedback;

❑ Explore techniques for overcoming biases and stereotypes;

❑ Practice skills for conflict resolutions;

❑ Identify methods for solving communications barriers;

❑ Help others overcome resistance towards those who are different.

Support Material: 288-page Trainer's Manual; Participant Manuals for Each Module.

These are just a few of hundreds of training programs available. Call your BNAC training consultant to discuss how our training programs can help you achieve your business goals. Call 1-800-233-6067 today.

Training and Consulting Services

BNA Communications Inc. offers a wide range of training and consulting services customized to help you in many areas of workforce diversity, equal employment opportunity, and sexual harassment prevention.

From analyzing and defining the problem, developing the strategy, to implementing the solution, our nationwide staff of highly qualified consultants have a long track record of contemporary experience and success working with a wide variety of leading organizations.

Training and Consulting Services Available Include:

Diagnostics/Needs Analysis

Want an outside, objective opinion on how to address your training requirements? BNAC's consultants can help you assess your situation and/or training needs and plan a strategy based on their experience working with many other organizations.

Executive Overviews

Need to help sell, position, and/or show others in your organization the strategic business impact of an intervention? Our consultants can conduct briefings and/or prototype training sessions at your organization, answer questions, and help adapt a program to your particular needs.

Pilot Sessions

Want to really put a program to the test before full implementation? Pilot sessions, led by BNAC's consultants, can help you fully examine a program with key managers and further adapt it to your needs.

Instructor Training Workshops

Would you like to give your in-house trainers additional background to enhance the effectiveness of these programs? BNAC's Instructor Training Workshops, held at your location, or around the country, will give your in-house trainers extra content knowledge and training skills to maximize your return on the training investment. We can also adapt Instructor Training Workshops to your organization's unique needs.

On-Site Implementation

Like the program, but don't have time or the trainers to conduct these high-impact, sensitive, and organizationally-challenging seminars? BNAC's consultants are available to conduct these programs at your location or at any site you select.

Custom Program Development

Want a training program tailor-made or redesigned for your exact training needs? Our staff of content experts, consultants and award-winning production professionals are available to modify current materials or create entirely new video programs and printed materials based on your unique business culture and/or other requirements.

Call for More Information

Our Training Consultants are at your service to help you explore your unique requirements and develop strategies for solving your training problems and turning them into opportunities. All at no cost or obligation.

Call 1-800-233-6067 today.

About The Bureau of National Affairs, Inc.

The Bureau of National Affairs, Inc. (BNA) is America's leading publisher of labor and human resources information. BNA publishes more than 200 information services covering such areas as human resources, labor and employee relations, environment and safety, tax, legal and health care. Services are available in print, CD-ROM, and on the World Wide Web. For catalogs and other information call 1-800-372-1033.

BNA Communications Inc.
a subsidiary of The Bureau of National Affairs, Inc.
9439 Key West Avenue, Rockville, MD 20850
1-800-233-6067   Fax: 1-301-948-2085
http://www.bna.com/bnac

LEADERS IN DIVERSITY, SEXUAL HARASSMENT PREVENTION
AND BUILDING RESPECTFUL, PRODUCTIVE WORKPLACES